MY CUP
RUNNETH OVER

GIVING *and* GENEROSITY

MY CUP RUNNETH OVER

GIVING *and* GENEROSITY

CHAD BIRD

My Cup Runneth Over: Giving and Generosity

Published by:
1517 Publishing
PO Box 54032
Irvine, CA 92619-4032

Publisher's Cataloging-In-Publication Data
(Prepared by Cassidy Cataloguing Services)

Names: Bird, Chad, author.
Title: My cup runneth over : giving and generosity / Chad Bird.
Description: Irvine, CA : 1517 Publishing, [2022]
Identifiers: ISBN: 978-1-956658-14-9 (paperback) |
    978-1-956658-15-6 (ebook)
Subjects: LCSH: Tithes. | Christian stewardship. | Charity—
    Religious aspects—Christianity. | Generosity—Religious
    aspects—Christianity. | BISAC: RELIGION / Christian
    Church / General. | RELIGION / Christian Living /
    Stewardship & Giving. | RELIGION / Christian Living /
    General.
Classification: LCC: BV772 .B57 2022 | DDC: 248.6—dc23

Printed in the United States of America.

Cover art by Brenton Clarke Little.

Contents

THE CHURCH OF TAKING OR THE CHURCH OF GIVING?

Near a massive church stands a bulldozer, its diesel engine rumbling. Soon it will reduce this sprawling sanctuary to rubble. It's going to take some time and effort, but it will fall. It's going to take time because it wasn't built overnight; in fact, its foundation was laid long ago, its walls erected in the distant past. And it will take some effort because the church's spires and steeples stretch to the distant horizon. In the end, however, when all of it has been torn down, then and only then will people see a shocking truth: this church should never have been built in the first place.

Let me explain what I mean. This particular church is not a brick-and-mortar structure with pretty stained-glass windows. Rather, it exists only in our minds. It is a conceptual church, that is, a way of thinking about the house of God. It's a notion of the church as a place of grabbing and getting, of demanding and taking—taking your money, your time, and your freedoms. It's like a religious club in which you're expected to pay your membership dues or a rigid community where you must measure up by carrying your portion of the financial weight. That's the church that never should have had a foundation, much less become a massive, sprawling structure in the heads and hearts of so many people. You come to this church full and leave empty. You come free and leave shackled with guilt and shouldered with demands you'll never be able to keep.

It's the ripple effect of this take-take-take conception of the church where we see the most harm done. You see, it's bad enough for people to think of the church as greedy for more, but this conception spreads outward. It becomes the way people view Christianity and the Lord Jesus himself. Instead of Christianity being all about what

God has done for us and given to us in his Son, it becomes all about what we need to do for God and give to God. It is a dangerous, depressing reversal of who God is, what Christ has done, and why he founded the church.

For that reason, this booklet on giving and generosity may surprise you. Perhaps you picked it up, looked it over, and thought, "Oh, here we go again, more things for me to do. This will be page after page of directions for me on how to be a 'good Christian' by following all the right rules of charity and stewardship." If that's what you're thinking, this booklet will not only be a surprise but a most welcome one. If there is a core message in these pages, it is that Christianity is all about the God who, though he was rich, for our sake, became poor so that he might enrich us with his grace (2 Cor 8-9). It is about our Father, who is giving and generous toward us in Jesus Christ. In these pages, you'll find a refreshing, grace-centered perspective on stewardship that focuses squarely upon the cross and resurrection of Jesus Christ.

I

THE GARDEN WHERE EVERY DAY WAS CHRISTMAS

When a baby is still in his mother's womb, little does he know how much his parents are hustling and bustling to prepare for the day he will make his grand entrance into this world. There are nursery walls to paint with just the right color scheme so that from day one, his eyes drink in the array of beautiful colors in this world. There are decorations to choose, along with a crib, changing table, and rocking chair. At baby showers, friends and family provide essentials like diapers, a diaper bag, a stroller, onesies, bottles, and a car seat. A pediatrician needs to be chosen, along with the hospital where the baby will be born. And, of course, there's the big question of what this baby will be named. Those few months leading up to the baby's nativity are packed with activity as his mom and dad do everything they can to ensure that when he is born, everything is ready for their child.

Perhaps you've never thought of it this way, but much of the opening chapter of the Bible reads like this preparation period for a child's birth. God, our Father, is hustling and bustling to create an entire cosmos for his children. He decorates the heavens with the sun, moon, and stars that his children will need to illuminate and beautify their world. He pours out rivers, seas, and oceans and stocks them with fish. He fills the sky with birds; the earth teems with animals as tiny as ants and as huge as elephants. Every element in the universe, down to the finest detail, God puts in place during the first five days of creation. Then and only then, when the nursery of this world has finally been made ready, does he smile and say, "Let us make man in our image, after our likeness" (Gen. 1:26).

Let this shockingly wonderful message sink in: Our Father said to his Son and Spirit, "Let's make an entire cosmos, and one lush planet in particular, for our children." That means that the sun shines for us. The rain falls for us. The cows graze, the stars twinkle, and the earth sprouts grain, all on our behalf. The truth is that the world does revolve around us. God created it that way. Not that it might serve selfish ends, of course, but that, through creation, God might serve and protect and cherish us, his beloved sons and daughters.

David was so amazed that he wrote a psalm in which he marvels at humanity's exalted place in the universe. He asks,

> When I look at your heavens, the work of
> your fingers,
>   the moon and the stars, which you have set
>   in place,
> what is man that you are mindful of him,
>   and the son of man that you care for him?
>   (Ps 8:3-4)

In view of the grandeur of the cosmos, David feels so minuscule as to be inconsequential, even beneath the divine radar. But he continues with this burst of poetic excitement:

> You have made him a little lower than the
>> heavenly beings
>> and crowned him with glory and honor.
> You have given him dominion over the works
>> of your hands;
>> you have put all things under his feet,
> all sheep and oxen,
>> and also the beasts of the field,
> the birds of the heavens, and the fish of the
>> sea,
>> whatever passes along the paths of the seas.
>>> (Ps 8:5-8)

The writer of Hebrews quotes this psalm specifically in reference to Jesus, "We see him who for a little while was made lower than the angels, namely Jesus, crowned with glory and honor because of the suffering of death, so that by the grace of God he might taste death for everyone," (Heb 2:9). In

Jesus Christ, the second Adam, the saving head of the human race, we also are crowned with this glory and honor, for we live and reign in him. Just as the Father created humanity to "have dominion over the fish of the sea and over the birds of the heavens and over the livestock and over all the earth and over every creeping thing that creeps on the earth" (Gen 1:26), so, in Jesus, we are recreated as those who are crowned with glory and honor to be the kings and queens of the universe.

At this point, I suspect some of you might be feeling a bit skeptical. You're thinking, "Hold on a minute. How can we be the kings and queens of all creation? We're only a single cog in the vast machine of the universe. Okay, we're important, but we shouldn't exalt ourselves as the most important part of this vast universe." It is indeed true that we mustn't exalt ourselves to that position. But we haven't done that; the Creator of the heavens and the earth has done it for us. He fashioned us to be the lords of creation. Not that we might misuse and abuse creation, but that, as those who bear God's image and likeness, we might "be fruitful and multiply and fill the earth and subdue it and have dominion" (Gen 2:28). In direct contradiction to what we are so often told these days, we are in fact why creation exists. God did not need and still does not need the world; we do. We need the sun, moon, and stars. We need land, water, and vegetation. We need oxygen, minerals, and metals. We need it all. Therefore, to fulfill our needs, to enrich us with all the incredible gifts in this creation, the Lord fashioned the universe and put it in our laps as a father might hand a present to his child, as parents might prepare a nursery for their newborn. "The earth is the Lord's and the fullness thereof, the world and those who dwell therein" (Ps 24:1). And this earth and the fullness thereof our Father has given to us whom he created in his image and likeness, to rule over it responsibly and thankfully.

The main point is this: God created us so that he might have children upon whom to shower his gifts. In the Garden of Eden, where the Lord fashioned our first parents, every day was like Christmas. Presents of all kinds were spread under every tree, beside the waters, above in the skies. Every aspect of creation was a brightly wrapped gift that could be opened, and again each time, with the childlike shriek of excitement. Even the bodies of our first parents were presents; Adam was a gift to Eve, as Eve was to Adam. God was anything but stingy. He opened his hand and satisfied the desires of every living thing (Ps 145:16). Everything that God saw not only as good, but very good, he gave to his crowning achievement in creation: humanity.

Therefore, in the book of Genesis, we see the true genesis, the starting point, for understanding giving and generosity. It all starts with God, and it all ends with God. He is the alpha and omega of giving and generosity. "Every good gift and every perfect gift is from above, coming down from the Father of lights with whom there is no variation or shadow due to change" (James 1:17). And every good gift and every perfect gift our Father has designed for his children.

But this is certainly not how everyone thinks, nor has it been throughout the ages. We usually don't suppose the account of creation in Genesis 1-2 is a radical story, a countercultural narrative about humanity's central place in this world. But, in fact, it is. If you compare the biblical account to various creation myths common in the ancient world, one glaring difference is why humanity exists.

For instance, suppose we walked down a street in ancient Babylon and asked one of the people, "Why are you here? Why did God or the gods create you?"

They would respond with something like, "I am here because the gods needed me."

"What do you mean the gods needed you?"

"Before we were created, the lesser gods had to do all the work in creation."

"So the greater gods created you to be a worker? To relieve the burden placed on the lesser gods?"

"Yes, of course. Our primary purpose is to work for the gods. We worship them and provide them with food and drink. We exist to be their servants. That's why we are here."

Our Babylonian man on the street echoes what he (and his religious culture) confessed to be true about humanity. According to their creation myth (known as the Enuma Elish), humanity is (1) an afterthought in creation; (2) at the periphery of the story; (3) and formed not as the gods' children but as their servants.

We can hardly find a more contradictory message to what the Scriptures tell us about why we exist and why God created us. Far from being an afterthought in creation, men and women are *the* forethought in creation. They are why God uttered the first, "Let there be. . ." Humanity is why everything else was made. And Adam and Eve were not at the story's periphery; their creation is the very climax of Genesis 1. Everything leads to day six, when the Lord says, "Let us make man in our image, after our likeness." And most importantly, God does not form Adam and Eve to be his servants; he creates them to be his children. He is their Lord, to be sure, but more importantly—more exactly—he is their Father.

The account of creation in Genesis 1-2 is still a countercultural narrative about humanity's central place in this world. If you ask a New Yorker or Floridian the same question we asked the Babylonian man on the street, you'll get essentially the same answer: we exist to achieve things; we are created to serve; our lives are defined by our doing, our giving, our working. Even if they believe in God and sit in church every Sunday, they are likely to answer these lines. It all boils down to this: *their identity is established by what they do*. This "doing" may be very religious. It may involve serving in the church. It may redound to the glory of God. But if you strip away all the externals, you are left with one fundamental belief about why we are here in this world: God created us as servants, doers, and givers.

Of course, it is true that when the Father created Adam and Eve, he gave them work to do. They were to fill the earth, subdue it, and have dominion over all creation (Gen 1:28). When the Lord formed Adam, he put the man in Eden "to work it and keep it" (2:15). And Adam needed a "helper fit for him," so God crafted Eve from his rib to be that helper (2:18, 22). Our first parents did not kick back in Eden and snore their days away in a hammock hung between the tree of life and the tree of the knowledge of good and evil. They had their vocations, their places of service in this new world. So do we. We are spouses or parents, workers and servants of every variety. God has given us work to do and people to help, both inside and outside the church. We are not called to be lazy sloths who spend our lives being waited on hand and foot.

However—and this is of critical importance—*we must not confuse identity with activity*. Who we are is not defined by what we do. We may do lots of good things, and we certainly do lots of bad things. At times we serve God, at times our fellow man, and very frequently, we selfishly serve the person in the mirror. But neither the good we do nor the bad we do defines who we are. Rather, our identity is determined by the one who has created us, redeemed us, and given us a brand spanking new identity in his Son. Whether we are awake or asleep, working 24/7 or a comatose patient in ICU, a newborn infant or a retired octogenarian, a millionaire CEO or a homeless man on the street corner—who we are has nothing to do with these externals. We are the children of our heavenly Father in Jesus Christ and through his Holy Spirit. Our identity is rooted in the family to which we belong. We are sons and daughters of our Father because we are brothers and sisters of Jesus Christ. To be in the image of God is simply to be his child. When Adam fathered Seth, the Scriptures say, "he fathered a son in his own likeness, after his image" (5:3). To be in the image and likeness of our heavenly Father is essentially this: to be his child, as Seth was Adam's child. It is to bear the imprint of our paternity.

Paul puts it this way in his letter to the Galatians: "Because you are sons, God has sent the Spirit of his Son into our hearts, crying, 'Abba! Father!' So you are no longer a slave, but a son, and if a son, then an heir through God" (4:6-7). Earlier, he says, "[I]n Christ Jesus you are all sons of God, through faith. For as many of you as were baptized into Christ have put on Christ" (3:26-27). To be baptized into Christ is to put on Christ, to be clothed with him, enveloped by his presence so that our identity is bound up with his. Since he is the Son of God, we who wear him are sons of God. Since he is free, we are free. Since he is the chosen one of God, we are the chosen ones of God. We are not slaves, and we are more than servants; we are children because we are *in* the only begotten child of God, Jesus Christ.

Because we are in Christ, our identities are determined by who he is, not by what we do. Just as the Father created Adam and Eve as his children, so we are recreated in Christ to be the Father's children. And just as he gave all things to our first parents in the newly created world, so in the kingdom of God, "all things are yours, whether Paul or Apollos or Cephas or the world or life or death or the present or the future—all are yours, and you are Christ's, and Christ is God's" (1 Cor 3:21-22). All things are yours because you belong to Christ, and Christ belongs to God. In other words, the giving and generous God, our

good and gracious Father, has enriched us with
every imaginable blessing in Christ. We are a new
creation (2 Cor 5:17). And in this new creation, we
are kings and queens. Just as the Father formed
Adam and Eve so that he might have someone
upon whom to bestow his gifts, he has reformed
us in his Son that he might have children upon
whom to bestow even greater gifts. We are defined
by what we receive, not by what we achieve, by
divine generosity toward us, not our generosity
toward others. We are the blessed, gifted, beloved
sons and daughters of our Father in Jesus Christ.
That is who we are.

2

CURVED IN ON OURSELVES

We're all familiar with the importance of first impressions. Whether positive or negative, these impressions we receive from other people can color the remainder of our relationship with them. Sometimes, though not always, that first impression is a snapshot that encapsulates the entire personality of the man or woman we meet. It's as if we get to know them, what makes them tick, in those first brief moments we visit with them. That initial impression becomes the permanent stamp of identity. This is who they are, what they're about, and how they're going to interact with us. We gain that insight the first time we're around them.

First impressions in the Bible are frequently
like this as well. When we are introduced to a
character in the Scriptures, very often the author
indicates to us what kind of person we are meet-
ing. He's dropping hints about the future already
in the present. This first impression is intended
to be a lasting impression. And nowhere is this
truer than when we first come face-to-face with
humanity's primal enemy in the Garden of Eden.

As discussed in the first chapter, Adam and Eve
lacked nothing in Paradise. Our Father had given
gifts to them without number. It was like Christmas every morning. They had life and health, love
and beauty, food and drink. And they had each
other. Moreover, they had a peaceful, perfect relationship with their Father, who had provided all
of these blessings to them out of his abundance
of love. He gave from a generous heart, and they
received with thankful hearts. And our parents
also gave themselves to each other fully, unhes-
itatingly, out of love. There was no stinginess or
greed, for such evils could not exist in the hearts

of those at perfect peace with who they were and who their Father was.

We meet our primal enemy, the devil, in the mouth of a snake. He's co-opted one of God's own creatures to do his bidding. He is like that. He has nothing truly his own, so he's always hijacking what belongs to God, aping the Lord, and twisting the good things of creation to his own warped ends. We're told the serpent was "more crafty than any other beast of the field that the Lord God had made" (Gen 3:1). That Satan would choose a crafty animal is already indicative of what kind of foe we are dealing with. The devil's no fool. He's a streetwise, cunning adversary who specializes in ambushes. In this first impression, he reveals the most about himself in his speech. The moment he opens his mouth, he also opens up his plan for all of us to see.

Though Adam and Eve are most likely standing side by side (the "you" in this dialogue is always in the plural), the serpent directly addresses the woman. He says to her, "Did God actually say, 'You shall not eat of any tree in the garden'?" (3:2).

Pay careful attention to the way this question is crafted. The devil has three primary objectives in speaking the way he does. First, he seeks to convince Eve and Adam to doubt and ultimately disbelieve divine speech. If he can get them to question God's word, to move from asking "did God actually say. . .?" to affirming "God actually didn't say. . . ," he's won the battle. Secondly, he twists God's words to say something the Lord never said in the first place. Our Father never told Adam and Eve that they couldn't eat of any tree in Eden. Quite the opposite! He said, "You may surely eat of *every* tree in the garden"—all except one, the tree of the knowledge of good and evil (2:16-17). So the devil has taken a gift and turned it into a prohibition.

And now we come to the third and most important objective of the devil. He reveals in this final objective just about everything there is to know about how he tempts us. Lurking beneath this question that the devil poses to Eve is an accusation that God is holding out on his children. Here's what the devil is saying, "Did God really tell you that you can't eat of any tree in the garden? You know what? I've been around him, and I can tell you from experience that sounds just like him. He's a small-hearted, tight-fisted deity. He has everything he needs, but he won't give you everything you need. Oh, he'll never admit it, but he's a selfish, egocentric Creator. Here you are, surrounded by all these good trees, and he won't let you have any of them, right? What does that tell you? That he obviously doesn't have your best interests at heart. You can call him Lord and God and King, but the most fitting name for him is Scrooge."

Let's return to this tactic of the devil in a moment, but first, let's pick up the rest of their conversation. Eve responds to the devil, "We may eat of the fruit of the trees in the garden, but God said, 'You shall not eat of the fruit of the tree that is in the midst of the garden, neither shall you touch it, lest you die.'" (3:3). At first glance, Eve's response seems to indicate that she's answering well. The serpent's pulling no wool over her eyes. But then she tacks on this: "neither shall you touch

it." Scour the words of our Lord in Genesis, and
you'll never find this prohibition. Adam and Eve
were free to touch the tree, sleep beneath it, climb
it, and swing from its branches if that tickled their
fancy. The tree itself was a gift from God. Only the
eating of its fruit was forbidden. Eve's addition,
"neither shall you touch it," is a red flag. It indicates that, ever so slightly, she's begun to buy into
the idea that God is being chintzy with his gifts.
She is saying, "Not only is he keeping the fruit
from us; he won't even let us touch it!"

It's at this point that the devil goes for the jug-
ular. He says, "You will not surely die. For God
knows that, when you eat of it, your eyes will be
opened, and you will be like God, knowing good
and evil" (3:5). What happens next is well known.
"The woman saw that the tree was good for food,
and that it was a delight to the eyes, and that the
tree was desired to make one wise, [so] she took
of its fruit and ate, and she also gave some to
her husband and he ate. Then the eyes of both of
them were opened, and they knew that they were

naked. And they sewed fig leaves together and made themselves loincloths" (3:6-7).

In his opening question to Eve, the devil introduces the notion that God is uncharitable, that he hasn't given them what they need and deserve. In his closing statement, he says God is lying to them to prevent them from having the full life he enjoys. "God knows…" the serpent says. "God knows that if you eat this fruit, you'll be like him. And he won't stomach that. He's like that mean, little rich kid who won't let anyone else play with his cool toys. Eve, let me tell you about this cheap, miserly God. He's been lying through his teeth. He made this world for himself, not you. All this stuff is for his own sake. You're not his child but his slave. He wants to keep you down low, under his feet. He's built this fence around the tree of knowledge and hung 'No Trespassing' signs because he knows that, if you eat of it, you'll be just like he is. So you show him. Take and eat. God is not giving and generous; he is greedy and grasping."

Many of you know this story from Genesis 3. Perhaps you know it well. The real question is

whether you look down and see your feet standing in Eden's soil. The truth is that we are just
as much a part of this narrative as Adam and
Eve are. The enemy that we first meet here is the
enemy that we confront on a daily basis. The first
impression he gives is the impression he continues to give in our encounters with him. And the
response of Adam and Eve is, unfortunately, our
ongoing response as well. You see, Genesis 3 is
our story, the unveiling of who we have become
because of who we have made God out to be. Like
our parents, we have believed the lie that God is
not giving and generous, that he is holding out
on us. And because of that, rather than trusting
in him to provide us with all we need to support
us in this life, we think and behave as if we are
self-providers, self-supporters, who can take care
of ourselves in this world. In short, we have made
ourselves into little make-believe gods who rule
our own little make-believe worlds.

Our struggle with giving and generosity is one
symptom of a much larger and deeper problem we
face. Martin Luther aptly described our condition

when he said we are *curved in on ourselves*. This inward curvature, this radical me-focus, affects us in both vertical and horizontal ways. Vertically, it cuts us off from our Father. Rather than looking up to him, being open receptacles ready and eager to be filled with his gifts, we transform ourselves into closed pots, impenetrable vessels that pretend we don't need God, that suppose we are doing just fine without him and his gifts. Horizontally, it cuts us off from our neighbor. Rather than looking toward them, being open receptacles ready and eager to pass on the gifts we have received from God to those in need, we clutch them as if our very life depended upon our possession of them. Like the ring in *The Lord of the Rings*, these possessions are our "Precious," which we will do anything to keep. So both in relation to God and to our neighbor—to God in faith and to our neighbor in love—this navel-gazing is destructive.

The ultimate struggle we face, however, is not so much that we are unwilling to be givers, that we are uncharitable, but rather that we believe that God is. This is of crucial importance. The origin of the problem is not merely that we have broken a law or violated a moral statute. The heart of the problem is this: we don't believe that God is our Father, that he loves us, that he gives us boatloads of gifts, that he wants nothing but the best for us. All stinginess, all selfishness, all the bad we see inside ourselves and in our actions with others—all of that is traced back to the false belief in a small-hearted, tight-fisted God. *The lack of human generosity is directly proportional to our perceived lack of divine generosity.* If I fully believe God is love, I will fully love others. If I fully believe God gives good gifts to me, I will fully give good gifts to others. But if I doubt that, if I suppose that I must fend for myself, take care of myself, then I will turn away both from God and from others. I will gaze at my navel as I curve in on myself, looking neither to God in faith nor my neighbor in love. And that is what we do. Like Adam and Eve, we think God is holding out on us, that he has not made us kings and queens of creation but abject servants who must take what they want when they want it.

In discussing giving and generosity, therefore, and why this is such a struggle, it is vitally important that we grasp the fundamental reason we struggle. It's a question of the lie that lurks in the human heart, a lie that has permeated and corrupted our entire nature, a lie that has wrecked our relationship with God and our neighbor. In Eden, we bought into the lie that says God is something besides good. In this untrue version of God, our Lord is transformed into a tit-for-tat deity, who is good to us only *if* we are good, *if* we are generous, *if* we serve him. In this lying depiction of God, he is a bookkeeping Lord who keeps a running tally of how much he will reward or punish us, depending on how well we measure up to certain standards of obedience. This lie about God reimages our Father into our Boss. Every day is not Christmas but another Monday morning in the sweatshop of this world where you have to earn your own way, pull yourself up by your bootstraps, and always be looking out for number one.

The fundamental reason we struggle with giving and generosity is the same reason we struggle with relationships, with work, and with every aspect of our lives: because, even as Christians, part of our nature still clings to a false god. This idol is the God who is not love, does not love us, and hasn't provided us full and free salvation in Christ Jesus. This idol is a false god who is curved in on himself. So our hearts respond the same way, by curving in on themselves. We reflect the image of the false God in whom we believe.

At this point, you may be thinking that we need a spiritual re-education program in which we are taught how to be better, more giving, more charitable people. If people are curved in on themselves, we need to gradually un-curve them and bend them outward by teaching them how to be more obedient. But that is not what we need; it is the direct opposite of what we need. The more we tell people to be giving, the less giving they will be. The more we demand generosity, the more tightly they will cling to their possessions. The more we preach that we must be unselfish, the more selfish we will become. *The most successful way to make someone worse is to continue demanding they get better.*

What we need is a substitute, someone to take our place, to pay the debt we owe. We need the true God, our loving and giving and generous Father, to make amends for our wrongdoing. In so doing, to fill us with a love that keeps no record of wrongs and makes no demands but gives and gives and gives some more. As we shall see in the next chapter, that is who God is and what he does for us.

3

THE OFFERING PLATE
IS TOO SMALL FOR
GOD'S GIFT TO US

We all want to have happy and healthy relationships. Husbands and wives desire a strong,
loving marriage. Friends want to get along with
each other. Parents desire to be close to their
children. When these relationships are at their
best, we enjoy them the most. As long as things
are going well, however, their deeper character
remains unknown to us. But when something tests
the relationship, we begin to see how true it is.
Most everyone, for example, has had fair-weather
friends who vanished when they could no longer
profit from the relationship. When marriages are
stressed by financial struggles or health issues,

some spouses throw in the towel and walk away. How we react to the strains and stresses of a relationship is a window into our commitment to the other person. And nothing reveals more clearly how strong that commitment is than when the other person can offer nothing in return.

Well, almost nothing. There is, in fact, one situation that reveals even more clearly how fragile human relationships can be: when the other person justly deserves not love but anger, not blessing but punishment from us. When they have wronged us, misused us, and trampled our love underfoot. When the whole world would back us in our urge to walk away, forget them, and leave them to wallow in their guilt and shame. In other words, when our friends turn into our foes, when our spouses betray us, then and only then is the relationship stretched to the max. I don't need to tell you that most of us walk away, don't we? We give up on them and the relationship. No matter how committed we might have been, no matter how faithful we might have been, some betrayals are too much for us. We see no other option than to end the relationship.

But it's not only human relationships that are tested this way; God's relationship with us, his children, was also stretched to the max. Think back to where we left Adam and Eve—and ourselves—in Eden. There was no good gift that our Father had withheld from us. We had his love, we had each other, we had a pristine world. We were living, quite literally, in Paradise. Yet we came to believe the lie that God was withholding something from us, that, in fact, he was by nature stingy. So we abused his love by acting as if he were self-serving. We were like people living in a mansion of gold who just had to get their hands on the one copper penny God had withheld. When we did, when we consumed the forbidden fruit, we immediately tasted the shame and death and accusation in our mouths. We patched together a flimsy covering of leaves to hide our nudity. Instead of seeing God as a giving and generous Father, we ran and hid from him like criminals from the police.

The looming question is this: How would God react to our rebellion? We had wronged him, misused his gifts, trampled his love underfoot. We justly deserved nothing but punishment. He could have rained down fire and brimstone on Eden. He could have screamed and yelled and disowned us. Or he could have looked at us, hiding in shame, shaken his head, and walked away, never to return. He could have done many things to end the relationship and our existence. But what he chose to do instead reveals everything there is to know about God, his love for us, and his unbreakable commitment to us.

The first words he speaks to us are a question, "Where are you?" (3:9). In Hebrew, it's a single word, but in that one word is squeezed a world of hope. In asking "Where are you?" our Father is inviting us to return to him. He's not playing hide-and-seek with us. He knows where we are. He knows what's happened. He knows that we have rebelled, broken his word, misused his love, and shattered our relationship with him. But knowing all that only makes him want us to return to him

even more. He doesn't want us living in shame
and death. He wants to restore the relationship.
So he beckons us out of hiding, back to himself,
with repentance in our hearts and upon our lips.

At this point, however, Adam and Eve still
have eyes only for their sin. Adam admits that
he's afraid of God. He and his wife feel the pres-
sure of their own guilt and shame, so they begin
to play the blame game. "The woman whom you
gave to be with me, she gave me of the fruit of the
tree, and I ate," Adam says (3:12). He thus shifts
the blame not only onto Eve but even onto God,
who gave Eve to him as a gift. And Eve, following suit, plays the-devil-made-me-do-it card as
she claims, "The serpent deceived me, and I ate"
(3:13). This response is typical of us when we are
initially confronted with our sin, isn't it? We're
sorry not so much because we did something
wrong, but because we got caught and because
of the consequences that follow. As we feel the
burden of guilt rising, we try to lessen the burden
by making excuses, pointing fingers, and claiming
extenuating circumstances.

Once more, however, our Father reveals his true heart. Yes, he goes on to tell our parents that the realities of earthly life have drastically changed because sin has now sunk its teeth into this world. Eve will writhe in birth pangs. Adam will work his fingers to the bone farming stubborn soil. There will be pain and sickness and strife and eventually death. This is simply what sin does. It spoils a splendid world. But more importantly, our Father speaks a word of light into the midst of this darkness. He foretells hope and healing and restoration. He promises that he will send the seed or offspring of the woman to crush the head of the serpent who has deceived them (3:15). This seed, this promised one, will bring down his heel upon the devil's skull with a force weighted with heaven's saving will. Humanity's enemy will be destroyed. Yet this destruction will also mean death for the seed. For the fangs of the satanic serpent will penetrate the heel of the promised deliverer. He, too, will die, even as Adam and Eve will die. Yet in his death will be victory over the grave, for he will have destroyed death by death. He will bury the grave.

What is almost as remarkable as this promise itself is the context in which it is spoken. All the labor that God has painstakingly performed to craft this masterpiece of creation for us, we have ruined. All the love that the Father has exhibited in making us, blessing us, treasuring us as his children, we have trashed. The relationship that our Lord has established with us, we have severed. And even when confronted with our sin, we have pointed accusatory fingers at others and even at God himself. Yet, despite all this, in full knowledge of everything we've done, our Father seeks us out, woos us back, and tells us that he is willing to send his Son to die in our place. We have made ourselves into his foes, yet he speaks to us as friends. We have acted like we don't even know him, yet he addresses us as his children. When our relationship with our heavenly Father was stretched to the max, he stretched out his arms to save us, forgive us, and draw us back into his healing embrace. Indeed, he promised that his Son would stretch out his arms upon the cross to die in our stead, to crush the head of our mortal enemy, and to recreate us as his own.

In the last chapter, we talked about being curved in on ourselves. We made the point that what we need is not a spiritual re-education program to un-curve us. Commands that tell us to be better, to be more giving, more charitable, more obedient, and less selfish are not going to help. Precepts are powerless to effect true change in us. In fact, they end up constantly accusing us for falling short. What we need is our loving and giving and generous Father to make amends for our wrongdoing. What we need is a stand-in, someone who says, "I've got this covered." That act of sacrifice will fill us with a love that keeps no record of wrongs, makes no demands, but gives and gives and gives some more. That is what we have in the seed promised to Adam and Eve, the seed who is the Son of Mary and the Son of God.

Jesus Christ did not come down from heaven to transform us into generous people. He was not conceived within the virgin Mary to conceive within us a charitable heart. He did not pour out his lifeblood so we might empty our wallets into the offering plate. He never said, "I'll do X, so they'll do Y." In other words, there were no ulterior motives for the life and death and resurrection of Christ. His purpose was not to make us better people, better givers, and better servants. He came not to transform us, but to be transformed into our sin so that we might be declared righteous in his eyes. "For our sake [God the Father] made him to be sin who knew no sin, so that in him we might become the righteousness of God" (2 Cor 5:21). God does not love us and save us because he can then get something out of us. He created us so he might have children upon whom to shower gifts. And he redeemed us for the same reason: that he might flood us with forgiveness, wash away our sins, give us his Spirit, declare us his saints. All we have to offer God are our sins, and he takes them away in the sacrificial death of his Son. We have nothing good to offer God. Nothing. Yet he gives us everything, including himself.

Indeed, so great is the love of our Father that
we gain more in Christ than we lost in Adam. In
our first father, we had original righteousness,
but in Christ, we have the righteousness of God
himself. In Adam, we were created in the image
of God, but in Christ, we are recreated in the very
image of the God who assumed our image in his
human conception and birth. In Adam, God was
our Father, but in Christ, God also becomes our
Brother. We are physically united to God in the
physical body of his Son so that we can truly say
that we are bone of God's bone, flesh of God's
flesh. No greater, more intimate union is possible
than our union with our Father, through Christ,
and in his Spirit. The relationship we broke, God
has restored. In his generosity and love, he gave
us his Son. And "he who did not spare his own
Son but gave him up for us all, how will he not
also with him graciously give us all things?"
(Rom 8:32). Indeed, because we have Christ, we
have all things. "All things were created through
him and for him. And he is before all things, and in
him all things hold together" (Col 1:16b-17). This

Son who made all things, who remade all things in his death and resurrection, had made us his own. We gain more in him than we lost in Adam.

The love the Father gives us in Christ is not proportional to our love for him. His giving and generosity are not reciprocal to our giving and generosity. It's the exact opposite. While we had no love for God, he loved us fully. And even after we become his own, and strive to love him fully, and always fail, he nevertheless continues to love us fully. His is the kind of love that does not look for someone worthy of love but loves even before it looks. He gives to us not as an investment but as a gift, pure and simple. He's not looking for a return on his investment because it's not an investment. It is pure, no-strings-attached charity. We are like beggars with open palms into which our Lord places his wealth. He doesn't do it to make us obligated but to say to us, "Here is my gift. I give it to you because I love you."

The offering plate is too small for our Father's gift to us. His generosity is not a tithe, 10% of his possessions. No, his gift is as large as he is, for he is the gift. He doesn't fill an offering plate for us but fills the womb of Mary, fills the cross, and fills a tomb with the joyful shout of his triumphant resurrection. He gives 100% to us, who can give nothing in return.

This is the Gospel, the Good News of our liberation in Christ Jesus. It was a liberation promised in the aftermath of humanity's fall in Eden, a liberation accomplished when the heel of the woman's seed fell upon the head of the serpent at Golgotha. It is finished. Salvation is accomplished. More than that, salvation is ours. Forgiveness is ours. All because Christ is ours. He has made us his own, given himself to us. And as we will discuss in this next chapter, he has taken up residence inside our bodies so that he can continue to do his work of love and giving through us.

4

WE ARE THE MASKS
OF CHRIST IN OUR
VOCATIONS

We've been hiking our way through the peaks
and valleys of the biblical story. Before we proceed, let's pause, turn around, and drink in the
view. There is the cosmos, as vast in scope as it is
breathtaking in intricacy—and every aspect of it,
great and small, God made for us. The universe
is the revelation of his universal love. Creation is
his generous gift to humanity. He made us not
for himself but out of himself, out of the love that
he himself is, for God is love (1 John 4:8). This
creation was fractured, and humanity was broken when we rebelled against the goodness of
our Father. We swallowed the lie that he is not

generous but a scrooge-like deity. We curved in on ourselves and thus closed out both God and each other. But our Father, rich in mercy, giving by nature, gave us even more. He sought us in our sin, called us back to himself, and provided the seed—his Son—by whom we are reconciled to him. He liberated us from a slavish life of self-service, self-getting, and self-justifying. We are free and forgiven. In Christ, we are recreated as the children of our Father, those for whom he made the world.

So, where do we go from here? Now that God has accomplished all of these great things for us, do we then proceed to live a life in which we accomplish great things for God? Having received his grace and mercy in Jesus Christ, do we move on to a life of obedience by walking in the way of his commandments? God gave to us; now it's up to us to give back to God, right? Empowered by the cross, we march forth into a life wholly devoted to him, right? Actually, no. That is not where we go from here.

The Christian never leaves the cross. It is not merely the starting point on our journey of faith. It is the beginning, the middle, and the end. The cross *is* the journey. It is where our new identity, our new life, is established and remains. Paul expresses it this way, "I have been crucified with Christ. It is no longer I who live, but Christ who lives in me. And the life I now live in the flesh I live by faith in the Son of God, who loved me and gave himself up for me" (Gal 2:19b-20). When we are crucified with Christ, when we die and rise with him in the waters of baptism (Rom 6:3-4), we are in Christ, and he is in us. We have no self-understanding apart from him. We have no identity apart from him. "It is no longer I who live, but Christ who lives in me." We are not empowered by a cross left behind; we are joined to our Lord upon it. And in the crucified Christ, we remain.

This means that the life we live, we live in Christ, and he in us. Our entire life takes on a cruciform pattern, the shape of a cross. I am a son, a husband, a father, a worker. You are children, too, as well as spouses, parents, friends, co-workers, and neighbors. Yet in all our interactions with others, in all our duties at home and work, whether we stand in the pulpit or sit in the pew, all of this we do not do alone. We have been crucified with Christ. And just as God was hidden in that man on the cross, so he is hidden in us. When we work, Christ labors in us. When we give, Christ gives through us. We are his hands, his feet, his mouth, his ears, for we have died and our life is hidden with Christ in God (Col 3:3).

One of the most liberating aspects of the Gospel is that we are freed from trying to win divine favor by what we do. "Without faith, it is impossible to please him," but by faith in Christ, we are already pleasing to him (Heb 11:6). He stands in no need of our good works. He doesn't need our money or time or anything else. Everything is already his, for "the world and its fullness" belong to him (Ps 50:12). Yes, we speak of offering things to God, but as David says, all we are doing is handing back to God what he has already handed to us: "All things come from you, and of your own have we given you" (1 Chron 29:14). In Christ,

our Father has done everything, absolutely everything, to reconcile us with himself. He doesn't
need our time, our talents, or our treasures.

But we do have time, so what do we do with
it? We have talents and treasures, so what do we
do with them? Once more, it is not a question of
what we do but what God in Christ does through
us. And here is what he does: Christ wears us like
a mask so that he might be of service to others
through us. In other words, God doesn't need
our time, talents, and treasures, but our neighbor
does. Therefore, Christ is at work in our lives to
will and to do his good pleasure of serving others
in us and through us as the masks of his love.

We are the masks of our Father's love in the
vocations he has called us. There, we no longer
live, we no longer work, but Christ works in us.
Just as giving and generosity cannot be understood apart from the giving and generosity of
our Father toward us, so his giving and generosity through us cannot be understood apart from
vocation. So what exactly is vocation?

Let's revisit our parents in Eden for a moment to answer that question. There they were, enveloped by the gifts of God, all bestowed on their behalf. Our Father created everything in six days, then rested on the seventh day, but his work didn't stop there. Indeed, Jesus himself says, "My Father is working until now, and I am working" (John 5:17). But how did (and do) our Father and his Son continue to work? They work through those who serve as their masks in creation. The Father worked and kept the Garden of Eden through Adam (Gen 2:15). He exercised dominion over the fish, birds, livestock, and all the earth through those who bore his image and likeness. He began to populate the world not by making more humans from dirt, as he did Adam, but through the intercourse of husbands and wives. In other words, God continued his creative work by means of his created children. He did not retreat into the nosebleed seats of heaven and sit there as a spectator to see what would become of his world. No, he stayed on earth and put on the masks named Adam and Eve so that in and through them, he might continue his generous, giving work on earth.

Our Father labors in this world and the church, utilizing our vocations. A vocation is simply a "calling." This calling includes our careers but is much broader than what we do for a living. God has placed us in multiple vocations. To be a son or daughter is a vocation, as it is to be a mother or father. Marriage, too, is a calling. To be a preacher or hearer of God's word is a calling. And, of course, to be a real estate agent, soldier, electrician, or teacher is a vocation. In each of these callings, Christ is at work in different ways to uphold and sustain the world. He doesn't act directly but works through these means or channels to dole out his gifts. Does God feed the world? Yes, but he uses farmers to sow and reap the harvest, truck drivers to haul the produce to market, grocery store workers to sell it, and chefs to prepare it. Does Christ preach the Gospel, baptize, and celebrate his Supper? Yes, but he uses churches to call and support pastors and pastors to engage in the ministry of giving out the saving gifts of God. Does God rule this world and protect us from evil? Yes, but he uses soldiers and police officers, judges and lawyers, presidents and governors as his masks so that he might watch over us through them. In each of these callings, God is hidden behind a unique mask. He is invisibly working through these visible means to give us the gifts of love, mercy, protection, and justice.

Our vocations are the spheres in which Christ is active in our lives to use our time, talents, and treasures for the good of our neighbors. Peter puts it this way: "Above all, keep loving one another earnestly, since love covers a multitude of sins. Show hospitality to one another without grumbling. As each has received a gift, use it to serve one another as good stewards of God's varied grace: whoever speaks, as one who speaks oracles of God; whoever serves, as one who serves by the strength that God supplies—in order that in everything God may be glorified through Jesus Christ" (1 Peter 4:8-11). Each person has received unique gifts; to be "good stewards of God's varied grace" is to use those in service to others in our vocations. But this service is "by the strength that God supplies." As Paul says, God "works in you, both to will and to work for his good pleasure" (Col 2:13). We are not free agents, doing good in the world, engaging in charity, as if this were our work. We have been crucified, buried, and raised with Christ. Our bodies are the temples of the Holy Spirit. The Father has made us his children. We are agents of the Trinity, his hands, feet, mouths, and ears in this world. Through us, in our vocations, God manifests his love for others.

This also means that our Father has made us dependent on one another. This flies in the face of our stubborn will to stand alone. "I can handle this. I don't need your help. I'm a do-it-yourself kind of person; I don't want to rely on someone else." All such independent sentiments, while quite American-sounding, could not be more anti-biblical. The very first thing God said was "not good" was the isolation of man: "It is not good that the man should be alone" (Gen 2:18). Adam needed a woman to whom he could give himself wholly. He needed a companion to whom he could be generous in love. Nor would it have been good for Eve to be alone, to have her own personal Eden where she was isolated from Adam. Humanity was created for community. We need each other. And we serve each other in our vocations, for in these callings, we give the gifts of God and receive from others the gifts of God. A radical claim of independence is an affront to our created reality. He made us to be children dependent upon him. He made us as those who give and receive love, help and serve one another in the vocations where God has placed us.

We see this dependence on one another, this giving and receiving of love, manifested in the life of the early church in a variety of ways. Immediately after Pentecost, the believers in Jerusalem "were together and had all things in common. And they were selling their possessions and belongings and distributing the proceeds to all, as any had need" (Acts 2:44-45). Later, when the believers in Jerusalem needed assistance, the believers in Macedonia and Achaia were pleased "to make some contribution for the poor among the saints at Jerusalem" (Rom 15:26)—Gentile Christians thus served Jewish Christians. Paul urged the Corinthians to complete their contribution to the saints: "Your abundance at the present time," he told them, "should supply their need, so that their abundance may supply your need, that there may be fairness" (2 Cor 8:14). He also adds that "each one must give as he had made up his mind, not reluctantly or under compulsion, for God loves a cheerful giver" (9:7). In all these situations, and in situations like them today, the Father manifests his love by caring for those in need, by supplying what they need, through others. There is no shame in dependence, just as there is to be no selfish boasting in generosity. Indeed, just as Christ is the hand that gives the gift to those in need, so Christ is also the hand to whom the gift is given. As he says, "Truly, I say to you, as you did it to one of the least of these my brothers, you did it to me" (Matt 25:40).

The glaring omission in far too many discussions of stewardship within the church is the central work of Christ in our lives via the vocations to which he has called us. "I have been crucified with Christ," we say with Paul. "It is no longer I who live, but Christ who lives in me" (Gal 2:19-20). What does this mean vocationally? It is no longer I who am my wife's husband, but Christ who is her husband in me. It is no longer I who am a father to my children, but Christ who is their father in me. It is no longer I who work for my neighbor in my job; no longer I who contribute to charities; no longer I who put money in the offering plate; no longer I who feed and clothe the homeless; no longer I who give of time, talents, and treasures, but Christ does all of these things in me. Our vocations are fully enveloped by him and his presence. We are the masks of Christ. This does not make us robotic. We are not simply going through the motions, having our strings pulled like puppets. Rather, we have been joined so intimately to Jesus that what he does, we do, and what we do, he does.

This is the freedom that the Gospel gives and creates within us. It liberates us from a life in which we try to earn divine favor by what we do. Our Father is already fully pleased with us in Christ. No more must be done. It has already been finished on the cross of Christ. God doesn't need every good deed, dollar, and hour of service that we might offer. Therefore, he directs it elsewhere, to our neighbor. And as we shall see in this next chapter, the faith that is active in love is a fountain of good works that never stops flowing.

5

THE SIMUL WAR
WITHIN US

For every person, there are at least three types of biographies that could be written. There is the autobiography. Because this is my story, as told by me, we might assume that this is the most complete and accurate version. After all, no one else has walked in my shoes. Only I have savored the sweetness of my successes and choked down the bitterness of my failures. So if anyone is qualified to tell the real story of me, it's me. And if it's an honest autobiography, it will include not only the good but also the bad and the downright ugly things I've done. No room would be allowed for photoshopping the picture I portray of myself.

There's also the biography that someone else could write about me. This may be a well-written account, but the fact remains that no matter how exhaustively the author might study my life, interview me, and attempt to get inside my head, his perspective will always be that of an outsider. Maybe he'll spotlight the good I've done, perhaps he'll drag my skeletons out of the closet to parade them before the world, or maybe he'll present a balanced approach. Whatever this author does, however, he'll tell only part of the story. Ultimately it's my story, not his.

But there is also a third option. What makes this story of me unique is that most of it reads like wildly exaggerated fiction. First of all, it's a version of my story that's so heavily edited I hardly recognize myself in its pages. Yes, the facts are accurate: dates of birth, marriage, birthdays of children; the schools I attended; the jobs and careers I've had. All those are included. But every single bad and downright ugly thing I've done is blotted out. And not just that. All the seemingly good things I did from a gross mixture of pure and impure motives are portrayed as having been done for the most pristine reasons. But still,

there's more. This story of my life includes details
of which I have little or no memory. Helping people I don't even recall knowing, much less assist-
ing. Feeding people, clothing them, visiting them,
speaking kind words to them. Every chapter in
this biography is packed with such stories. After
reading it, you'd think my life had been sinless,
holy, and perfect.

And that's the point. For this third type of biography is penned by our Father, who sees us exclu-
sively through the lens of his Son, Jesus Christ.
Who we are, what we've done, why we've done
it—all these are filtered through the purifying
blood of Jesus. He retells our story as his story.
Our biography merges with his. Because of that,
the story of us that the Father writes is actually
the most complete and accurate version, for we
are completed and made right in Christ. We were
crucified with Christ, so our biographies are no
longer ours but Christ's living in us by faith.

The ongoing struggle we face in this life is this:
God's biography of us we know only by faith,
whereas our autobiography, as well as what

others see in us, we know all too well by experience. God in Christ says we are righteous, but
we see our hearts are fat with faults and failures,
our souls saturated with stinginess. Our Father
declares us to be saints in light, but we know
that in the darkness of sin, we feel right at home.
Even when we contribute to charities, for instance,
or give to the homeless or drop some money in
the offering plate, our actions are anything but
wholly pure. Unless we're deceiving ourselves,
we know this to be true. A stew of selfless and
selfish motives stirs within us. For instance, we
may give money to the church, but why? Yes,
we do it to support the work of the kingdom,
but don't we also do it to soothe our guilty con-
science, to be looked upon as generous, to use it
as a tax write-off, to make us feel more righteous
than those "tightfisted non-tithers," and the list
goes on. When we're honest with ourselves, all
our giving and generosity, no matter how huge
or tiny the amount, is prompted by a heart that
beats inside a selfish sinner.

During the Reformation, this inner tug-of-war between good and evil was summarized by the Latin phrase *simul justus et peccator*, which means "simultaneously justified and a sinner" or "simultaneously saint and sinner." It is an inner simul war between the *old me* and the *new me in Christ*. It's a war involving giving and generosity as well as every other part of our lives. In his letter to the Romans, Paul describes this daily war in detail. Listen to this refreshingly honest description of his life:

"I do not understand my own actions. For I do not do what I want, but I do the very thing I hate . . . For I know that nothing good dwells in me, that is, in my flesh. For I have the desire to do what is right, but not the ability to carry it out. For I do not do the good I want, but the evil I do not want is what I keep on doing. Now if I do what I do not want, it is no longer I who do it, but sin that dwells within me" (7:15-20).

Bear in mind that this is not how Paul was before he became a Christian; this is the apostle speaking of himself *as a Christian who is simultaneously*

saint and sinner. And it is who we are as well. We
want to be giving, for instance, but our greedy
fingers clutch at our possessions. We want to be
generous to those in need, but the stingy self-serving actions we do not want is what we continue
doing. The inborn, sinful nature within us, which
Paul calls the "old self" (Rom 6:6; Eph 4:22), is a
recalcitrant mule that digs in its heels and will not
change, will not improve. It is, and will remain
until death, selfish and rotten to the core. It is
the *peccator* in *simul justus et peccator*.

Finally, Paul cries out, "Wretched man that I
am! Who will deliver me from this body of death?"
(7:24). It is our cry as well. Who will save us from
ourselves? Who will rescue us from our insatiable
appetite for getting more for ourselves, from our
coveting of what others have, from our love of
money, from the motley mixture of motives that
compel all we do? Who will deliver us?

Before we get to Paul's answer, notice that he
does *not* ask, "*What* will deliver us?" There is no
program of spiritual improvement that you can
follow to come out on top in this struggle. There

is no ten-step guide to living a victorious Christian life in which we overcome our selfishness and greed. There is no "what" that delivers us. There is only a "who."

Paul tells us who this is: "Thanks be to God through Jesus Christ our Lord!" (7:25). He and he alone delivers us from this body of death. He and he alone rewrites our biographies so that they mirror his own. He puts to death our old sinful nature by drowning that enemy in the flood of baptism—the same waters that crucify and bury us with Christ (Rom 6:3-4). And he raises us anew, in his own resurrection, that we "might walk in newness of life" (6:4). This new life is not a victorious Christian life in which we begin keeping the Ten Commandments. It is Christ in us. It is the life he lives in our vocations, as discussed in the last chapter. It is the life that God the Father sees when he sees us. Jesus does not initiate an improvement program within us so that we're eventually good enough, generous enough, giving enough to pass muster with God. Jesus simply forgives us. He gives us himself. He strips away

our filthy rags, puts them on himself in his crucifixion, and clothes us with his own righteousness.
He becomes as we are so that we become as he is.
He becomes the sinner atop the cross so that we
become saints in him.

The good news—the best news ever!—is that
God our Father loves us just as we are. He is the
only one for whom "I love you" is a complete sen-
tence. For us, it's always

"I love you . . . for I find you worthy of my
    love.
"I love you . . . because you love me.
"I love you . . . but I will stop loving you if
    you hurt me.
"I love you . . . but I love someone else more."

With our Father, it is simply, "I love you."
Period. "God shows his love for us in that
while we were still sinners, Christ died for us"
(Rom 5:8). While it is certainly true that "God
loves a cheerful giver" (2 Cor 9:7)—and we pray
for those cheerful hearts—he also loves a less-
than-cheerful, reluctant giver. He doesn't love the

cheerful giver because he is cheerful, nor does he
love the reluctant giver because he's half-cheerful.
Our Father is love, does love, and will continue
to love because that's who he is. His is that one-
way love that gives to us when we have nothing
to offer in return.

Perhaps you're thinking, "But shouldn't we
respond to God's love by being giving and generous people?" Yes, we should, but notice that when
we speak this way, we have thrown ourselves
right back under the bus of the law. The moment
we add "should" or "shouldn't," "must" or
"mustn't," "shalt" or "shalt not," we are speaking
the language of command, of that which requires
something of us. All such language is accusatory
because the law always accuses. It always finds
fault, for it always finds something lacking within
us. The fingers of the law never cease wagging
at us.

The beautiful truth of the Gospel is that, in Jesus
Christ, we *are* giving and generous people, for we
have died, and our life is hidden with Christ in
God. There is now no condemnation for us for

we are in Christ Jesus (Rom 8:1). When our Father
sees us, he sees only his Son. He sees all our less-
than-perfect works as perfect in Christ. He sees
all our less-than-generous giving as perfect giving
in Christ. He sees all our failed attempts at being
faithful spouses, loving parents, good friends,
helpful neighbors, and responsible employees
not as failed attempts but as flawlessly executed
good works well pleasing to him. Why? Because
we are not flying solo. All we do, in word and
deed, is done in and through Christ. In him, our
F becomes an A+. On the cross, he dealt with all
our failures. There he finished it, once and for all.
We became new creatures. We were reformed into
the image of Christ. Our bond with him is as close
as skin to skin, bone to bone, blood to blood, for
all of who we are has merged with all of who he
is. Therefore, the law cannot accuse us anymore.
The Gospel has liberated us from every effort to
please God by our works. He is pleased with us
in Christ. Nothing will change or improve that.

   We do need to hear the law. We need to be
admonished "to do good, to be rich in good works,

to be generous and ready to share" (1 Tim 6:18). We need to hear that "whoever sows sparingly will also reap sparingly, and whoever sows bountifully will also reap bountifully. Each one must give as he has decided in his heart, not reluctantly or under compulsion, for God loves a cheerful giver" (2 Cor 9:6-7). We need to be warned that "the love of money is a root of all kinds of evil" (1 Tim 6:10). The Spirit uses these words to instruct us as to the way we should be, the kind of heart we should have, the evil inclinations we ought to avoid. And the Spirit uses these words to reveal that we have lived up to none of these requirements. Not one. Not one single time have we used our time, talents, and treasures as we should, as God demands.

Therefore, we admit our failures, we pray the Spirit may create in us a charitable heart, and we flee for refuge to the infinite mercy of our Father. That mercy is a bottomless treasure chest. "For you know the grace of our Lord Jesus Christ, that though he was rich, yet for your sake he became poor, so that you by his poverty might become

rich" (2 Cor 8:9). The Father has ransomed us "not
with perishable things such as silver and gold, but
with the precious blood of Christ, like that of a
lamb without blemish or spot" (1 Peter 1:18-19).
The Father welcomes us like the prodigal son,
asking no questions, making no requirements,
just welcoming and embracing and loving us as
if we are the most special treasure in the world
to him. Because we are. We are, like Israel, his
"treasured possession" (Deut 7:6), the "apple of
his eye" (Ps 17:18), those for whom God was willing to give the life of his Son to save.

This love of the Father in Jesus Christ has its
way with us. It creates within us a desire to mirror that love in our dealing with others. When
Jesus loved and accepted the chief tax collector,
Zacchaeus, that man who once had cheated and
defrauded for a living, turned around and said,
"Behold, Lord, the half of my good I give to the
poor. And if I have defrauded anyone of anything,
I restore it fourfold," (Luke 19:8). Jesus didn't
require this generosity of him. And if Zacchaeus
had given nothing to the poor, he still would have

been loved just the same by Jesus. But when Jesus loved and welcomed this undeserving man whom society largely rejected and hated, he responded to that love by sharing his wealth with others. That's what the Father's love does. It flows into us and through us into others. We become the vessels through whom the Father bestows more and more of his love on our neighbors. There is no law in this. It is simply the fruit of the Spirit; it is the result of faith. As Luther says in his Preface to Romans, "O it is a living, busy, active, mighty thing, this faith. It is impossible for it not to be doing good works incessantly. It does not ask whether good works are to be done, but before the question is asked, it has already done them, and is constantly doing them" (*Luther's Works*, American Edition, 35:370). That's because, in faith, Christ is present and active, doing his work in and through us. And where Christ is, he is not idle but actively loving and giving.

The simul wars within us, in which we struggle between the old nature and new nature, is a conflict that Christ has already won for us. "We have peace with God through our Lord Jesus Christ" (Rom 5:1). Why? Because "we have been justified by faith" (Rom 5:1). That justification is a completed action. We are declared pure and forgiven and righteous in the eyes of God. He has drowned the old sinful nature and raised us anew with Christ. We are new people, fresh creations crafted from Christ himself. He has given all to us. He has been astonishingly generous toward us. He has held nothing back. "He who did not spare his own Son but gave him up for us all, how will he not also with him graciously give us all things?" (Rom 8:32). That is what we have in Jesus Christ: all things. All mercy, all forgiveness, all grace; full adoption into the Father's family; complete holiness and righteousness in the Holy Spirit; a cup overflowing with the treasures of the kingdom of God.

That is our biography: the true account of us as written by the Father, using the pen of the Spirit, dipped in the crimson ink collected at Calvary.

CONCLUSION

THE DEFINING MARKS
OF CHRISTIANITY

We began these reflections upon giving and
generosity with a church that needed to be bull-
dozed. It is the conceptual church, a way of thinking about the house of God as if it's a place of
grabbing and getting, of demanding and taking.
This misconception of the church, Christianity,
and our Lord Jesus is an understandable confu-
sion. Far too many times the sweet proclamation
of the Good News of Christ has been soured into
a set of spiritual demands or moral requirements.
People have been given the impression that the
church is where you come full and leave empty.
You come free and leave shackled with guilt and
shouldered with demands you'll never be able
to keep. Our giving and generosity have been

portrayed as if they are the defining marks of Christianity. They are not.

The defining marks of Christianity are found in the palms of Christ. His hands are imprinted with the marks of the nails by which he, because of his love for us, was bound to the cross. In the giving of his life for us, in his generous outpouring of blood upon the tree, we see the defining marks of the faith. This faith is in a God who never stops loving us. He created an entire cosmos for Adam and Eve and us, their children. Even when we rebelled and wandered away from him like lost sheep, he went searching for us, found us, and carried us home on his shoulders. He hasn't given us 10% or 50% or even 99% of himself, but all of who he is. He himself came down from heaven, impoverished himself by taking on our debt of sin, then enriched us with the wealth of his crucifixion and resurrection grace. And he joins us to himself. He crucifies us with himself, buries us with himself, resurrects us with himself, so that where he is, there we are. Where he is active, there we are active. In our vocations he himself is present, to continue to love and give toward those in need. Though we still struggle against sin and temptation, his Spirit fights for us and within us. That Spirit brings forth in our lives the fruits of Christ himself. This is the message of the church—the church where Christ is present to give us more and more of himself.

Everything we are, everything we have, belongs to God. "In him we live and move and have our being" (Acts 17:28). And this is the best of news. For in God we have not a tyrant, not a demander, but a loving and gracious Father. In his Son, Jesus Christ, we have a brother, one who shares our flesh and blood, prays for us, and dwells within us. In the Spirit, we have communion with the Father and the Son. We are members of the family of God.

We are who God wants us to be in Christ. We are where God wants us to be in Christ. Surely goodness and mercy shall pursue us all the days of our lives, for we are the beloved of God in Jesus Christ. In him our giving and generous Father fills our cup of blessing until it overflows.

9 781956 658149